Also by Ronald Wallace

Poetry

Plums, Stones, Kisses & Hooks (1981)
Tunes for Bears to Dance To (1984)
People and Dog in the Sun (1987)
The Makings of Happiness (1991)

Poetry Chapbooks

Installing the Bees (1977)
Cucumbers (1977)
The Facts of Life (1979)
The Owl in the Kitchen (1985)

Criticism

Henry James and the Comic Form (1975)
*The Last Laugh: Form and Affirmation in the
    Contemporary American Comic Novel* (1979)
God Be with the Clown: Humor in American Poetry (1984)

Anthology

*Vital Signs: Contemporary American Poetry from the
    University Presses* (1989)

Time's Fancy

Ronald Wallace

University of Pittsburgh Press
Pittsburgh • London

The publication of this book is supported by grants from the National Endowment for the Arts in Washington, D.C., a Federal agency, and the Pennsylvania Council on the Arts.

Published by the University of Pittsburgh Press, Pittsburgh, Pa. 15260
Copyright © 1994, Ronald Wallace
All rights reserved
Manufactured in the United States of America
Printed on acid-free paper

Library of Congress Cataloging-in-Publication Data
Wallace, Ronald.
   Time's fancy / Ronald Wallace.
      p.   cm. —(Pitt poetry series)
      ISBN 0-8229-3868-5 (alk. paper).—ISBN 0-8229-5548-2 (pbk. alk. paper)
   I. Title. II. Series.
PS 3573.A4314T5 1994   94-21670
811'.54—dc20   CIP

A CIP catalogue record for this book is available from the British Library.
Eurospan, London

The author and publisher wish to express their grateful acknowledgment to the following publications in which some of these poems first appeared: *The Antioch Review* ("The Resurrection and the Light"); *Apalachee Quarterly* ("Canzone: Siesta Key"); *Artful Dodge* ("1959," "Sweet Corn"); *Boulevard* ("Poison Ivy"); *Cincinnati Poetry Review* ("The Inaccessible"); *The Georgia Review* ("Pastoral"); *Kansas Quarterly* ("Beethoven and the Birds: The Piano Trio in C Minor," "Cricket"); *Kentucky Poetry Review* ("Ballade of the Humpback Whales"); *The Laurel Review* ("Canzone: Egrets," "Man and Machine," "Saints"); *The Nation* ("Ballade of David Parsons," "Quick Bright Things"); *Poet & Critic* ("Hunger"); *Poetry* ("February 14," "The Furnace Men," "Grandfather, His Book," "Hardware," "The Life Next at Hand," "The Swing"); *Poetry Northwest* ("Ballade of the Orangery," "Honky-tonk," "Pantoum: The Sturdy of Worry," "The Physics of Marriage," "The Story,"); *Prairie Schooner* ("Running"); *Shenandoah* ("Ballade of the Recycling Center"); *Sou'Wester* ("Strips"); *Tar River Poetry* ("In the Cards"); and *Yankee* ("A Valentine"); and *Yarrow* ("The Astronomy of Loss," "Dragonflies").

"Ballade of the Humpback Whales" originally appeared in *Kentucky Poetry Review,* vol. 27, no. 1 (1991). "Earthly Pleasures" was first published by the Phi Beta Kappa Society in *The American Scholar,* vol. 61, no. 4 (Autumn, 1992). "The Failures of Pacifism," was originally published in *Looking for Your Face* (New York: Orchard Books, 1993). "In the Cards" originally appeared in *Tar River Poetry,* vol. 29, no. 2 (1990).

I wish to thank the Wisconsin Arts Board (in conjunction with the National Endowment for the Arts), the Dane County Cultural Affairs Commission (in conjunction with Madison CitiArts and Madison Community Foundation), and the Graduate School Research Committee of the University of Wisconsin-Madison for their generous support.

Epigraphs excerpted from W. H. Auden's "As I Walked Out One Evening" are from *Collected Poems* by W. H. Auden, Copyright ©1940 and renewed 1968 by W. H. Auden. Reprinted by permission of Random House, Inc.

Cover Art is a reproduction of Paul Klee's *Fish Magic,* reproduced by permission of the Philadelphia Museum of Art: Louise and Walter Arensberg Collection.

Book Design: Frank Lehner

for Margaret

*And Time will have his fancy
To-morrow or to-day*

—W. H. Auden

Contents

1

The Life Next at Hand	3
Cricket	4
The Failures of Pacifism	5
Earthly Pleasures	6
The Astronomy of Loss	8
Pastoral	9
Beethoven and the Birds:	
The Piano Trio in C Minor	10
Quick Bright Things	11

2

February 14	15
Sweet Corn	16
Dragonflies	17
The Physics of Marriage	18
Tricks	19
The Theory of Relativity	20
Canzone: Siesta Key	21
Ballade of the Orangery	24
Hunger	25
Why I Am Not a Nudist	26
A Valentine	28

3

The Story	31
The Swing	33
The Sins of the Fathers	34
1959	35
Honky-tonk	36
Strips	38
Poison Ivy	39

Hardware	40
Ballade of David Parsons	41
The Resurrection and the Light	42
Running	43
The Inaccessible	44
Saints	45
Canzone: Egrets	47

4

Pantoum: The Sturdy of Worry	53
The Furnace Men	54
Man and Machine	56
Why God Permits Evil	58
Ballade of the Recycling Center	59
Possum, 1942	60
Exploration and Discovery	61
Sentences: A Play in Five Acts	62
Ballade of the Humpback Whales	64

5

Dream Lanes	67
Teachers: A Primer	68
In the Cards	73
Grandfather, His Book	74
Personal Effects	75

1

As I walked out one evening,
 Walking down Bristol Street,
The crowds upon the pavement
 Were fields of harvest wheat.

The Life Next at Hand

Behind a camouflage of sticks and debris
we once mistook for a sparrow's routine intrusions
a house wren is building
her nest in the Shopper Stopper box.
Every day when the mailman,
driving, left-handed, his beater,
leans as far into her life as he can,
she gives him what-for in a song.

I have reached in more than once myself
to pull some tiresome sparrow out
of a place meant for something better
before I've found that small cup of promises—
a puff of the tiniest grasses, a twist of snakeskin—
behind the wordy camouflage of the commonplace.

Cricket

*Ooooh, you've got gigantic cockroaches
in here!* the girls shout. They're fifteen,
out to the country for the first time and
unnerved by insects, chickens, cows, and dirt.
I hear a shoe clapped like a hammer
to the floor, getting that misapprehension
unmistakably nailed down.

How fear and inexperience become us.
How wealth and ease send our small wits
packing, or keep us always out at recess
from the school of hard knocks, armed
to the teeth with self-deception.

I could go on. I've had my own
rattlers in the backyard, bats in the belfry,
monsters in the closet, wolves behind the door.
Nevertheless, when I scrape the broken cricket,
all rust and silence, contorted residue of song,
off the kitchen floor, I say a small
elegiac for our history, for us all.

The Failures of Pacifism

When our milk goats and their kids cavorted
into a dark nest of mud daubers camouflaged
in the high grass of August, and danced
their dance toward oblivion, their tough skins
a sizzle of ripple and twitch, their sweet
faces swollen, one eye cordoned off from
the other, one nostril Picasso-like, comic, askew,
their udders all elbows and knuckles,
precarious balloons,

                    my daughter,
the vegan, and animal-rights activist, who,
like certain Tibetan monks or Hindus,
would sweep the path in front of her
as she walked so as not to step on
the least of this world's sweet creatures,
heartsick and outraged, surreptitiously
commandeered a large can of Raid
from the dark garden shed, and nuked
those ancient demons mercilessly,
dispatching them and their mad offspring
to the scrutiny of history
and the land of kingdom come.

Earthly Pleasures

The young cat, a dervish
of fur, plagues
the old cat, a dishrag
of familiarity. The young cat
is perpetually leaping
on the old cat's back,
harassing its dreamy nights,
flaying its misplaced days.
They race around the house,
pursued and pursuer,
in some ancient assignment
of catch and fetch.
The old cat could, of course,
bat the young cat
into kingdom come,
and dispose of the bloody evidence,
but it won't, for reasons
locked deep in the species.
Instead, it occasionally
commandeers a ladder-back chair
and from there
taps at the young cat
as if in a child's game of
I got you last,
the young cat humbling
itself, turning its vulnerable
belly up for the slapping,
the old cat an indifferent deity.
Lewis Carroll notwithstanding,
cats never smile, their

expressions stolid, unchanging.
Is there pleasure for them
in this? Or frustration? Or just
nothing—an occasion like
breathing or salivating. Does
the sunflower lust for life?
Does burdock cower
at the sound of the decapitating scythe?
Does the dark earth shudder
at how hard we work
to put it and us asunder?

The Astronomy of Loss

I bumbled through the night
with its sudden encumbrances
of door frame, wheelbarrow, and pump,
lugging my clumsy instrument.
Out here in the country
there is dark enough to see
the planets and farthest galaxies—
M31 in Andromeda, Hercules' globular cluster,
the rings of Saturn and moons of Jupiter
spoon in the cup of my scope.

If everything lopes across the field
of vision, it isn't the universe moving,
it's us, hurrying past
to our separate destinations,
thumbprints smudged on the glass,
the heat of our perceptions just
a matter of spin and tilt.

The lights in the house are out.
Their familiar constellations
grow faint with distance as midnight
snaps on its black lens cap
and packs up. As if change
were a precision instrument
of polished mirror and glass,
and loss the only landscape
that could be dependably called up.

Pastoral

They say it was an absence of cows
that brought this old barn down,
twisted the stone foundation
against itself until the king beams,
swaybacked and woozy, cracked under
the strain of so much dry air.
Moisture, our neighbor farmer,
leaning back on his heels, said. *Moisture*

and heat would have saved it. Sweet
Jesus! What must it take,
in these late days of our ransacked
lives, to save what's left of longings
on which we put everything down?
Who'll off to market, singing *cows, cows?*

Beethoven and the Birds: The Piano Trio in C Minor

The birds were pretty damn good.
On my back porch in Richland County,
the sky breaking up in fast-
moving clouds after the first
rain in days, the birds were
tuning their errant instruments
up for the evening concert: the tremulous
warble of wren and oriole, the vibrato
of field sparrow and finch, the slow
piccolo of chickadee, the trill
of catbird and cardinal, an oboe
of crows. Even the shy bluebird
lifted its tentative flute.

Meanwhile, inside the packed house, the boom
box rose in volume, as Beethoven
sashayed on stage, lifting his wily baton.
And then it was dueling virtuosos:
the silly violins flittering,
the tinny piano a-twitter,
the scored cello soaring
from thicket to runnel and rivulet,
feathers iridescent in the sun.
And for one glorious moment—Oh!
the improbable harmony, the whole
disturbed world turning, every
headstrong musician in tune. And then,
the birds returned to their twirping.

But Beethoven, Beethoven
danced by the light of the moon.

Quick Bright Things

And it is in September that beauty,
forsaking its tenacious footholds,
the durable and clumsy insistencies of summer,
takes its most tenuous shapes—
swallowtail, aster, cricket, and switchgrass—
as if to tell us it doesn't care
to put up the slightest resistance, as if
to say delicacy, evanescence, and meekness
are an end in themselves, and radiance flows
to those who with grace and disinterest
let go.

    May the armed potatoes hunker
in their bunkers of dark, the roots and tubers,
rammed into their silos, give no ground,
the skunks and weasels hold their tedious sleep
against heaven, we'll go with the sweet
scent of wood smoke, the brief season of leaf-
mold and midge, the short-lived, the perishable
quick bright thing. Against the permanence
of darkness and silence, we'll spin out
a tenuous deliquescence. We'll sing.

2

And down by the brimming river
　I heard a lover sing
Under an arch of the railway:
　'Love has no ending.'

February 14

How time expands
to map the lost occasion:
A kiss, say, on the doorstep
of your sixteenth year,
that valentine to the future
that will always be arriving
at whatever address you've paid for
with such bright currency.

Or, likewise, contracts:
A decade, maybe, shrunk
to a scrap of paper,
an unintelligible scrawl
on the face of a torn envelope,
a message never sent.

Sweet Corn

You were all vinegar and regret,
the heat in the cold room rising.
I was trying to eat sweet corn, finding
it hard to remain fundamentally
serious—the cob on the clumsy lips,
the smack of a typewriter platen
clacking in the back of the mind's
old cartoon, the melted butter dripping
slowly over the chin, the shreds
of kernels wedged in the yellow teeth.
If it came down to a choice between
winning the goddamn argument, or finishing
my corn, I was stymied: I was angry,
my temper at a boil, but sweet Jesus
I was hungry, and somewhere, only
hours ago, in the green days of summer,
I must have loved you, marriage a great
harvest, a field you could get lost in,
all weed free and abundant (give or take
a row) and so I bit my salty lip
and oh, I know it's corny, gave in
to love and the sweet self-deprecation
of corn of corn of corn.

Dragonflies

Look, she said, *a whole platoon
of dragonflies.* He thought she meant
a squadron, since they were airborne,
but he was airborne, too, and so he said
nothing, just looked up from her nude
body, half in shadow, half in sun,
in the small clearing on their secluded
ridge, a warm day in mid-September.
The piercing blue sky was trying to say
something about death, the maple leaves
exploding in the branches, the small flak
of acorns on his back. There was a lull
in the action as she slipped out from
under him, hovered, and then was sliding
down on him and down, as the dragonflies
droned on above them, and they carried on
as if they were a company, at least,
if not yet a division, a battalion.

The Physics of Marriage

I know that the gold in this ring
is the offspring of the explosion
of some dark star ten billion years ago
when the atoms went shimmering off on
their long voyage that would pause here
to flicker on your finger as if
it were somehow substantial, and not
just a casual addition of electrons

in a probably indifferent emptiness.
What theory is there to explain us?
How we accelerate through our half-lives
toward these moments of exquisite collision
making what new particles visible
to the most untutored, elementary eye?

Tricks

FOR C.L.L. 1946–1992

The devil said, *pick a card, pick any card,*
you won't believe this trick. I picked
the ace of hearts. The devil said, *good,*
and tore the heart in half and slicked

back his black hair. *I know that it's absurd*
he said, *but I do love this trick.*
Now look what you've got left, just look!
The heart fell to the floor, a crippled bird.

Now let's say that's your heart, he said.
And God, it was my heart. *And now let's say*
you're me, he said. I was—my lover dead,
my heaven and all its angels passed away,

their torn voices burning in my throat:
Now you see it; now you don't.

The Theory of Relativity

Suppose you'd never known that at forty
boredom and rage would replace desire
in love's frantic panoply, that,
as your body's sense of time changed,
the world, like Einstein's train traveling
at the speed of light, would return one day
to find you inconceivably aged,
moving too slow to keep up
even the semblance of appearances,

would that first kiss on the doorstep
of your sixteenth birthday, the summer
breeze waiting for you to breathe
back the despair that would carry it
through to autumn, have had the power to
pull you back and back along the abandoned
track with its small prairie fires
started by the sparks of a past
that was once, and was once again, your future?

Canzone: Siesta Key

Our first view from the condo of the beach at Siesta Key
was of sand, whiter than our untanned skin, whiter than snow.
We had been told it was the loveliest of the keys,
though perhaps not so picturesque or artsy as Key
West, perhaps more restful. We were given to believe
that, under the circumstances, rest was the key
to recovery. Stripped to swimsuits, the condo key
clipped to our basket, we walked out into the Florida heat,
past the bright bougainvillaeas, the palmetto palms, the heated
pool, through the powder white sand, cool as a brass key
on our feet, the unlikely sun burning a hole in the sea,
the slate blue and flaming sea.

I'm not sure what, robed in cold, we wanted from the sea.
Perhaps it was enough just to know we were here, with this key
element before us, and that whatever gifts the elusive sea
would give us would be enough. Who could possibly foresee—
coming from the North country, all that withholding and snow—
what a voluptuous invitation, what savory music, the sea
would offer us. How we would, walking, marvel at the sea
anemones wavering in tide pools, how we would almost believe
that they waved their bright stingy flowers at us, believe
the jellyfish, out on patrol, translucent as the sea,
could be calling us in out of this heavy heat,
this voluptuous, somnambulant, heat.

We thought we knew, after all, what we'd come for: heat,
and a few meditative days on the beach, by the sea.
Up North, there were all the cold shoulders, always the heat

of deadlines and schedules, the bicker of heartbeats, the heat
of muddle and puzzlement between us, for which there was no key.
Until, for all our pretense of desire, we proceeded without heat
day to day, with sex, that dark ray, our only undulant heat.
We might as well have thrown ourselves naked in the snow,
as tried to stay warm in that cold. Outside the snow
made a mockery of the radiant glow of the space heater
working away as weak and debatable as belief,
that false friend, that traitor, belief.

What could we then, lost even to ourselves, hope to believe?
In a cold landscape, where ten below is considered heat,
everything we'd hoped, in the flush of fancy's first belief,
to hold, fell to our crabbed imagination's distorted belief
that we'd never again need to think about the sea,
that love and luck were more than just words, were a belief
that could take us wherever we wanted to go. That same belief
that, dressed in the clothes of the moment, gave us the key
to the strongbox that held all our emptiness, the key
that clanged against the bell of our hard-cast belief
and cracked us past recognition, cracked us like snow,
like snifters of crusted snow.

For all the sunshine and ocean, we've brought our own snow.
It's the one thing in which we, despite all, believe.
Like drugged winter we grow high on it, this dubious snow
that shines through our silences, this familiar snow
that will not melt no matter the travel or heat,
the words and gestures and double entendres of snow,
the unspoken policies we have on each other, the snow

that's as vast as, stretching out from us, the sea,
where we know now we want to go. We step into the sea,
which freezes our toes, thighs, and shoulders, cold as snow,
as we wade out away from the warm shore, the key
fading behind us like regret, that door with no key.

Could we somehow become the world's great key
unlocking the past like a fortress of snow
and find inside what we need to help us believe
in this sonorous weather, this improbable heat,
this uplifting salt of the sea.

Ballade of the Orangery

Outside Sarasota, Florida, at this mom-and-pop
orange grove on the roadside, we stopped to pick
some Valencias and Temples, the last crop
lost to frost being loaded onto the beat-up truck
to haul away for juice. The bright citrus slick
with rime, the sun a seedy pulp, the dark rind
of dusk hung over us, as night with its dark wick
drew out the salty stars and we passed on

to grapefruits and tangelos, tart, sweet, your mop
of hair ruby in the moonlight, your voice thick
and sticky, your words sectioned on your lip
a sour reminder of our slow, then quick
decline. We stopped for a moment to suck
in the night air, hoping the grower wouldn't find
us stealing produce. Then, tongues out as if to lick
the salty stars, we drew apart and passed on

to other lives. You to a country you would swap
forever, and me to the cold North, thick
with ice and responsibility. Now, as I sip
juice from a hole cut in an orange end, or suck
the pulp of a grapefruit, or, musing, lick
the rim of a tangelo or halved lemon rind
on a frosty night, I find myself stuck
with the image of salty stars you passed on

to me that night in Sarasota, when our luck
ran out, as sure as if the grower with his gun
had finally found and salted us with buck-
shot, under the salty stars when you passed on.

Hunger

Satiated. Small globules of fat
flatten on the stoneware,
on the knives. The steak bones
blister with spittle. Shreds
of lettuce shrivel on the side dish,
potato skins wrinkle and die.

It is like the aftermath of war,
of sex, the spoils spoiling,
spoiling us, our neurons
overloaded, too satisfied to think
we'll ever eat another bite.

And what of love, of work, ambition?
We could laze in satiation all our days
blubbering about our rank good fortune,
full of ourselves and sick to death
of everything.

But luckily, we grow hungry, we grow
ravenous. Desire brings
the world back once again.

Why I Am Not a Nudist

FOR MARGARET, AUGUST 3, 1993

Mornings, I like to lie in bed
feigning sleep as my wife rises,
pads to the bathroom on her bare feet
in the rhythm that,
after twenty-five years of marriage,
I know by heart.

I like to watch, surreptitious,
my eyes still thick with sleep, her slip
out of her prim wool nightshirt,
and into her cotton panties—the half
knee-bend she does to pull them straight—
and the way her small breasts flatten
as she rears back and crosses her arms
to pull her T-shirt over.

She pretends not to know I watch her,
or how the still small pleasure
of the withheld sweet familiar
stays mysterious after all.
And if the day begins to fray
from grace toward consternation—
all that naked bickering—
imagination's raiment stays inviolate.

It is perhaps not unlike how what you
maybe once engaged in—in the heat
of passion, say, some small unspeakable

kinkiness you could hardly believe
you'd think of, and could not consider
afterward without embarrassment,
that nevertheless provided
such unlikely mutual pleasure—
must remain secret.

A Valentine

AFTER HEISENBERG

It is just good physics
how, merely by observing,
the observer changes the observed.
Not that I know much about physics,

but maybe the human heart
works on the same principle.
When William Harvey, the principle
discoverer of the heart's

motion, posited the pump
as metaphor, the poet
and scientist merged, and the poet
changed forever both pump

and heart. I am no scientist,
but love, look at this pump,
this heart; it pumps
for you sure as a scientist

changes the whole world
with his patient, loving
observations, sure as you, loving
me, would change the whole world.

3

But all the clocks in the city
  Began to whirr and chime:
O let not Time deceive you,
  You cannot conquer Time.

The Story

When we came out to the island
we didn't expect . . . ah,
that would be the way to begin:
a half-sentence of promise and mystery,
the delicious delay of gratification
at the end of each
anticipatory line; *When . . .*
the Western time frame, fixed, dependable,
with all its philosophical trappings—
cause and effect, progress, the idea
of heaven; *We . . .*
the invention of the self, the romantic
fiction of the individual within
democracy's improbable community; *Came . . .*
the active verb, graphic, decisive,
encoded with sexual reference; *Out . . .*
a kind of emergence, perhaps?
leaving the safety of the shore
and our old lives behind? *To . . .*
that innocent preposition with its
homonymal undercurrents that
tripped our childhoods up; *The . . .*
the almost invisible modifier,
incontrovertible article
of faith in the solidity and
particularity of things; *Island . . .*
the exotic setting, would it be
South Seas? or North Atlantic?
That self-contained isolating boundary
the tides ravish daily with their

intriguing cargo; *We* . . .
and by now we're friends,
dear reader, aren't we? The child's
thrill of excitement and abandon
in that ecstatic syllable; *Didn't* . . .
the off-handed contraction, informal,
conversational, masking its bipolar
opposites—assertion and negation,
push and pull, give and take,
the yes and no, the death that
defines the entrance; *Expect* . . .
and isn't that the heart of any story,
after all? Expectation and desire
the energy that attends every journey,
the gas that fuels the lobster boat,
the wind that fills the sails,
the sea that keeps us afloat toward . . .
What! the mind, hankering after arrivals,
keeps shouting through the morning fog.
Although it knows to know
the answer is
to kill the story off,
close it down so tight
no light or breath can enter,
leaving it, and us, no place
to go, yet it will
drive on regardless to its ending,
will demand to know.

The Swing

How could he know that that
moment, strung between his parents'
hands like some improbable bead, or part
of a chain that, for all he knew, extended
indefinitely into a world that seemed
large and untarnishable, would stay
fixed in his memory more surely than
any occasion of real moment. That
the definition of "momentous" would, in fact,
change as he aged down the years, spinning
the dross of his childhood to gold.
That his father would, eventually,
as all things eventually must, rust
through, and break his hold on him,
and his mother fray and snap
like the strand of nylon wiring
a cheap string of pearls, leaving him flat-
footed on the cracked sidewalk,
he who had swung free of gravity and time
in that one moment when he was too
giddy in the thin air of his
childhood even to notice.

And now in the days long with thought,
that kid has no use for him, isn't about
to stop his ascent into the heavens
he knows surely are there, as surely as
this moment, his moment,
will last at least forever.

The Sins of the Fathers

Because John, my paternal grandfather,
and a pretty farmhand named Ellen
begat my father out of wedlock
while John's wife hanged herself
from a rafter in the barn, my father
attributed his illness to their sin
and praised God for His mercy.
It was a strange theology
I never understood as I watched him
haul himself up the twenty-seven steps
to church every Sunday morning,
first on crutches, and then backwards
with his hands, on the worn seat
of his pants. The pastor,
from the pulpit, called it courage,
but the glow that came from me,
which the parishioners took for pride,
was rank humiliation, sheer embarrassment,
and finally anger: What kind of God
would punish passion so, with the sour
smell of urine and a central nervous system
fouled beyond repair like so much tangled
cable? And was it fair I had to live
with his infirmity, and embrace it
as my own, and be forever punished
with his loving me, as he loved God,
despite the fact that we had both
forsaken him?

1959

It was not a particularly good time
to be alive. Khrushchev was pounding his shoe
on the U.N. table: "We will bury you."
And I was unlucky at love. There seemed no rhyme
or reason. My father, stuck on crutches,
blundered through the house, akimbo. My mother
wept. And yet, that time, like no other,
loiters on the corner of my memory, clutches

the future in its sad hand. What is meaning,
after all, but the cohabitation of the past
with the present? How history, like some lost
lover, presses its diaphanous body, steaming
with joy and sorrow, down and down on you,
filling you with happiness. And then drowning you.

Honky-tonk

If our house had been a conch shell
held up to the wide ear of the ocean,
listing in the music of that great roar,
then my father had been the conch,
curling in his wheelchair
through its whorls and corridors,
attached somewhere in his study
by his slow, immoveable foot
as though no one could pull him out.

Years later, vacationing alone on Cozumel
in a hotel whose backed-up toilets
and disconnected phones could not disrupt
the Tecate and lime on the beach
under the thatched huts
with the sun in December snorkeling
through a sky blue as a marlin,
I was told by an oceanographer that
(in addition to the fact
that barracuda only attack
when they smell blood,
and my feet were abraded with coral)
you can hang them by their foot
all night on a line
and eventually they will tire,
simple muscle that they are,
and let go, unrolling
through their long eventless history,
exhausted. Or, you can just boil them.

But this was then, miles before Mexico
and my own conclusions,
as I coexisted in that house
with my father who would come
out of his study periodically
(if I held on long enough, or brought him
with all my honky-tonk to a boil)
to yell at me to *stop that awful racket
on the piano!* When all the time I'd thought
I was making music.

•

Strips

I found them in your dark cedar closet,
these gray metal canisters marked "strips."
Late one night, when you were out, the ancient
8 mm projector excitedly clattering, I watched:
the *Queen of Burlesque* in her bleached-out finery,
ironing her bra to the sway of amazing breasts;
the *Starlet* in the bathtub, her dark midriff and lips,
her Betty Grable hair-do, her soapy bump and grind.

Thirteen, stiff and dizzy, my heart and breath
erect, I was filled with wonder. Who were you,
Father, limp in your grimacing wheelchair, before
the myelin stripped its finery from your spine?
And why, thirty long years later, are we here
in spats and baggy pants, twanging our suspenders,
in this voluptuous clatter, this smell of cedar?

Poison Ivy

It was, she said—this exquisite
itch that stretched its prickly fingers
up her thighs to her crotch
and twisted languorously in
her pubic hair—like nothing so much
as an infinitely extended,
stretched thin as a rubber
band to the breaking point but
never snapping back, orgasm.

With the switch of her hand
she would slap it all night,
slap and tickle and twitch
in what must have been
(in another circumstance, an occasion
of briefer duration), ecstacy.

There is so much we can never capture:
the itch that language, with its
own delays and imprecisions,
can only locate with tropes,
powerful but approximate, the sentence
that ends unsatisfied in
some mystifying syntactical glitch,
as when my father, the most
patient of men, who, for forty years
suffered his long illness and our
mutual silence, reached up at the end
for my hand as if, suddenly,
loquacious, to scratch, or touch.

Hardware

My father always knew the secret
name of everything—
stove bolt and wing nut,
set screw and rasp, ratchet
wrench, band saw, and ball-
peen hammer. He was my
tour guide and translator
through that foreign country
with its short-tempered natives
in their crewcuts and tattoos,
who suffered my incompetence
with gruffness and disgust.
Pay attention, he would say,
and you'll learn a thing or two.

Now it's forty years later,
and I'm packing up his tools
*(If you know the proper
names of things you're never
at a loss)* tongue-tied, incompetent,
my hands and heart full
of doohickeys and widgets,
watchamacallits, thingamabobs.

Ballade of David Parsons

FOR MY FATHER, 1924–1981

The hall is dark and silent. The curtain rises
on an empty stage. But no, in the wings
David Parsons, naked to the waist, apprises
the situation. His loose pants, drawstrings
drooping rakishly, billow. He springs
three feet above stage level, and pauses there,
a strobe light catching him, catching him, taking
a casual stroll on the thin bright air.

Like an old movie, jittery, ridiculous, he despises
gravity. Charlie Chaplin, perhaps, walking
down the street in that best of his guises—
the sad tramp who leaves us laughing
at his jerky antics, his quicksteps, or crying
at the world's habit of handing out despair
to the sweetest and most innocent, the sting
of even a casual stroll, of taking the air.

But Parsons is carefree, big-hearted. He realizes
nothing, keeps walking, cane in hand, singing
a little tune as the whole audience rises,
smiling, like moons. I see my father swinging
on his manic crutches, just so, flinging
his arms and legs akimbo; and later the wheelchair
where, for ten long years, he sat, lingering—
even a casual stroll just so much thin air.

Dance, put him here. Coattails flapping, winging
across the quick, bright stage, happy, care-
free, as if, for all the world, singing!
As if taking a casual stroll on thin air.

The Resurrection and the Light

Because, after the age of twenty-two, my father
couldn't move a step without a cane,
then crutches, then a wheelchair, and worse,
I rise each morning, twice his age, and run

four slow miles through a congregation of corn,
past the foolish shit-bespattered cows,
to the country church, its stern spire
piercing the bright side of heaven

where my father thought he'd take up
residence one day, in white robes and light
on his feet as some celestial Fred Astaire.
He's buried there.

So every morning the slow dead wake up
and all the mired cows take flight.

Running

Jogging with my daughter to the point
through the bleak, denuded trees,
oak leaves rasping beneath our sodden feet,
I gaze at the lake, so blue and unforgiving
beside us, a pale hiss of mist
dousing the lit match of the sun,
a loon in the honeysuckle, giddy with our
intrusion, unfurling its whorled voice.

She tells me she hasn't had her period
for three months, now. "Running,"
she hazards, "or diet." And then,
"Why are boys like that?" she asks.
"They say they love you and then
you're their 'bitch' or 'cunt.'"
Her thin words burn, then freeze.

She says she believed everyone equal,
all desire and value the same, just
a matter of economy and season. Now
everything's changed. "Dad, were *you*
ever like that?" We're breathing hard now,
our even strides broken, the future
all glare ice and sleet. Overhead, geese

are keeping their noisy appointments,
inscribing the whitening sky
with their annual gray changes,
their accountable songs about snow.
And I think of this heartless season
when all of nature seems dead
set against us. And I don't know
what to tell her. I simply don't know.

The Inaccessible

They were standing at the edge
watching something in the foam and froth
of the gulf. Somewhere far out at sea
a storm was driving its hard message home,
while here its first thin syllables
were drowned in static. Their backs,
a blaze in the August sun, turned cinder.

What was it in the surf that so
engaged them? And multiplied itself
up and down the coast like jellyfish, like rays?
There are things in this dark world
that are better glanced askance at,
as stars clarify in the corner of the eye
and vanish in the clear light of day.
There are things better left unexplained.

In this eddy of trough and wave
nothing that surfaces stays.

Saints

I would not have thought that it
could happen to my own daughter.
But when she disembarks,
luminous, wafer-thin,
I am thinking of the medieval women
who were purported never to eat;
in all their transparent saintliness,
never to touch a morsel,
and so were closer to God
than any of the elders
with their tests and observations,
their theological speculations
over mutton and beef and a cool
tankard of ale at the local tavern,
who were prepared to pay alms to the family
for the privilege of watching God at work
whittling his thin creation down.
And could I be the anxious parent who,
implicated in the ruse,
would kiss a bit of sustenance back
into his hapless victim, a grape, perhaps,
lumped under the tongue, or
a prechewed wad of venison
lodged in the cheek and passed along
in that innocent affectation,
or the brother who, concealing
a bit of yam or sweet potato
in his homespun hankie,

would help his fairer sibling
blow her nose?
Who could be responsible for this?
Even Freud believed that women discovered weaving
by studying their own matted pubic hair
and could anything be stranger? And so,
when I reach out for my daughter
in the crowded airport
fat with the hustle and bustle of people
sliding through each other like grease,
the plane disgorging
its passengers and luggage,
my sharp arm hovering,
I pray that God, who wouldn't, after all,
let his people starve, who gave them
manna in the wilderness,
and a thicket stuffed with ram,
will reach out even
to a grieving nonbeliever
and will stay him.

Canzone: Egrets

Florida. The land of pig frogs and palmetto palms,
alligator hunts, wild hogs, anhingas, and egrets,
where in winter the sun is as close as the palm
of your hand, where fast-talking developers can palm
off almost any worthless piece of land in a cycle
as old as the swamps. When Ponce de Leon set palm
to ship's rudder, and, after six months saw these palms
for the first time—regaled with the promise of trails
to the fountain of youth, banking on mythical trails
of gold, the thought of all that wealth crossing his palm—
the months of salt, with nothing to drink but rain water,
must have paled in the face of such forage, such water.

Or did he see nothing but swampland, unreclaimable water,
the only gold in his life destined to be palm
nuts, the only fountain of youth this vast water
on which scrub vegetation flourished, this still water?
Or did all these mythical creatures, cormorants and egrets,
spoonbills and armadillos, great blue herons and water
moccasins, make it all finally worthwhile, his watered-
down dreams and expectations still more than the usual cycle
of disillusionment, that small pulse in the universal cycle
of losses. When God cast his shadow over the waters,
and the land rose, on fire, what immortal spore, what trail
did he leave for explorers to follow? What orisoned trail?

My daughter and I, fleeing winter, flew south, on the trail
of white powder beaches, fresh seafood, warmth, and water.
At Mayakka State Park, we followed a backpacking trail
through live oaks festooned with Spanish moss, a trail

rooted up by wild hogs over burnt, thriving palmetto palms,
back through decades of interlopers—hogs, palms, trail-
breakers like Ponce de Leon—as if we, too, were on the trail
of something more than anhinga or heron or egret,
as if we could walk beyond mistrust, loss, regret,
as if, pursuing our true destination, we didn't trail
this residue of the past behind us, part of that cycle
inescapable in this earthly life, that primordial cycle.

The next day, from a grizzled concessioner we rented bicycles,
vintage antiques, and, pedaling madly, tried another trail,
unhoused in the park. In the inevitable cycle
of seasons, we had been unable, for months, to bicycle
back in Wisconsin where the sun was ice, and water
froze even in imagination. We had been in a cycle
of silences, adolescence, and midlife crisis, cycles
that had become as familiar to both of us as the palms
of our hands, as sure as the lines in our palms.
We'd come here, unerringly, hoping to break the cycle,
hoping to walk through or ride down disappointment, regret,
let our love take wing like some exotic spoonbill or egret.

Outside our condo, each evening, we watched an egret
feed at the edge of the beach, following its ancient cycle
of fish, flight, and rest. What did it have to do with regret
in the blue dependencies of evening, this elegant egret
we dreamed of, making its insistent impermanent trail
on the beach, doing what, since the beginning of egrets,
it must do, just as we must make symbols of egrets.
If all of us, after all, originally rocked in water

not unlike the gulf, burst forth on the world out of water,
why shouldn't our desires and silences find in this egret
the same lines inscribed in our open, cupped palms,
the same futures strutting, clasped palm to palm?

Daughter, I give you the gold of my promise, my palm.
May your life rise up like a fountain, like an egret,
like the dreams of that madman, Ponce de Leon, the cycle
of his bright incorrigible quest, his unlikely trail
toward immortality, toward childhood, toward water.

4

In headaches and in worry
 Vaguely life leaks away,
And Time will have his fancy
 To-morrow or to-day.

Pantoum: The Sturdy of Worry

In the paper today I read [sic]
about "a sturdy of worry"
at the local psychiatric clinic.
They are prepared to pay money

to study the sturdy who worry
though there's nothing to worry about.
If they're prepared to pay money,
I'll sign up. I worry a lot.

Though there's nothing to worry about,
I'm continually sick to my stomach.
Signing up to worry—my lot
in life. No confidence. No pluck.

I'm continually sick to my stomach.
Meet anxiety, my oldest friend,
Mr. No Confidence, Mr. No Pluck.
But what if my anxiety ends?

If anxiety, my oldest friend,
at the local psychiatric clinic,
ends? *What if my anxiety ends?*
I read today's paper, worried sick.

The Furnace Men

Are too young. No more than
twenty, twenty-two. I had pictured
taciturn, grizzled codgers,
all wisdom and expertise. Not these
callow youths who, for all their
bright good looks and disarming
charm, don't seem to know
a cold-air intake from a flue.
They do not grasp
the language of sealed combustion,
plenum, condensate, or vent,
appreciate the meaning of a BTU.
Now they're turning on
their saws, and cutting out
this house's old heart
as I'm thinking ventricle and auricle,
chamber and aorta, how the world
can take us by surprise
with its strokes and complications,
as the years wear on
with their aging belts and pulleys,
their familiar sigh and wheeze,
heat exchanged for the cool
hesitations of loss and grief,
until we find ourselves helpless
under the weather, under the knife,
under the gun, with nothing
left to do but trust to

the innocence and energy
of the very young
who keep showing up
in all the places only we
used to know and be.

Man and Machine

The fat construction worker,
standing over the hole in the broken street,
is eating a peach. It is furry
in his hand, and thin juice leaks
from his tingling teeth.
Behind him, the green earth-
mover is lifting its stiff neck
and taking a bite of pavement. The machine
is thinking about how the sound
of crunching asphalt is sweet, how
the oils they spread on the macadam
smell like heat. The man
seems to be thinking
of nothing. The machine
sits back on its heels and eats
another peach. (Well, it's actually
a chunk of asphalt, but one
can always pretend.) The machine thinks
it has something stuck in its throat.
It thinks it is another man,
much like the man leaning over
the hole with the peach. The machine
feels kind of gravelly and hawks up
a wad of phlegm which it spits
into the hole. The man seems to think
nothing of it. *Okay,* the machine thinks,
it's pleasant on the street
in the furry afternoon,
my oiled bearings tingling.

The machine would just as soon
be working as sitting alone
in the silent yard all night,
listening to itself rust.
Meanwhile, the man is dreaming
(as nearly as he can be said to dream)
of being somewhere else. The street
is a mess. And the machine is acting up.
And here's another angry home owner
approaching, waving his arms.

Why God Permits Evil

At age eleven he seriously considered
cutting the hair from his sister's Barbie
and pasting it strategically on his pubes
to look in the sixth-grade locker room
more like a man. Instead, he hid in a corner,
and slipped from his obligatory jockstrap
straight into his stained BVDs
as the rest of us paraded in the showers
with what must have looked to him
like steel wool, woven mats, thatch.

Did he know we needed him?
Would always need someone like him?

It's not unlike the argument for why
God permits evil, without which who
could know or choose the good?
We've all been that small boy
stuck in the corner, assaulted by
the catcalls, hoots, and whistles,
which may explain the secret joy we feel
when the rich grow poor, the mighty fall,
and we give them all the sympathy
and comfort we can muster
across our phony faces.

Ballade of the Recycling Center

If the world were made of garbage—and it is,
so to speak, everything turning and returning
in the end—you'd never know it on this
bright, cold day: the new snow covering
the dump, its slow atrocious smoldering
a fever cooled; boils and pustules of trash
frozen under the season's light wing;
the world's dark refuse all sparkle and flash.

The attendant, wearing earplugs, his
jumpsuit stained and steamy, is singing
to himself, grinning foolishly as if he is
retarded, as if he's tickled we are bringing
our aluminum, plastic, waste paper, and tin
for him to crush in his compactor. The crash
of glass and cans unmans us as he spins
our world's dark refuse into sparkle and flash.

One day the whole world could be just fizz
and spittle, God, that glad attendant, flinging
our pop cans and newspapers into a bright whizz
of color, as, knee-deep in debris, cancer pouring
out of the sky, we find ourselves tossing
that one last pop top onto Dr. Eckleburg's ash
heap, that one last straw finally igniting
our world's dark refuse into sparkle and flash.

But today, the snow's a white page, promising
pure poetry, a clean getaway, balderdash
that, recycled through history, prompts us to sing
our world's dark refuse into sparkle and flash.

Possum, 1942

It's not unlike a big white rat, said the women.
It might have distemper or rabies, said the men.
Please, please, please, please, please, said the children.
And between them the matter was decided.

They gathered in our backyard and muttered with their guns,
fear chewing through them like some furtive hungry rodent,
their hushed words scrabbling, and foaming at the mouth.

When the shots came and the terror or excitement
rose and then folded into the looming afternoon,
the children, who would not soon forget the day's lesson,
lay upstairs, eyes tight, silent, playing possum.

Exploration and Discovery

Because the native women
in their immortal skin
favored the glint of metal
and the glint in
the eyes of any Caucasian,
Captain James Cook's men
on a Tahitian expedition

to triangulate Venus
in the great transit of 1769
pried so many nails loose
from the sailing ship
to buy their bit of heaven
that on the return trip
the ship almost went down.

It didn't. Left behind, the women
died of loss and smallpox. The men
went about their business
building lives and families
in London and environs,
their knowledge of the heavens
nailing the future down.

Sentences: A Play in Five Acts

1

Landing at Provincetown, and
finding no potable water,
the Pilgrims moved on to
Plymouth where, according to
the Indians, they bathed
but once a year, and fouled
everything.

2

Because it was
slow and floated so
conveniently when dead,
the right whale was
the "right" whale to kill.

3

The minke whale, always
considered too small to hunt,
and thus regarded with contempt,
has fast become the
favored prey of Japanese whalers
who, abiding by the ban
on commercial whaling, take
the whales for "scientific
research" before
putting the valuable
carcasses on the market.

4

To clean up Boston
Harbor, the city fathers
propose to pipe the
mostly purified
sewage (40 to 70 percent free
of toxic waste), out
to Massachusetts Bay, where
it won't disturb
anyone.

5

In the time it takes
to read this sentence,
one species will go
extinct, ten acres of
woodland will fall,
and one hundred babies
be born, and it's
too late now—
you've read it.

Ballade of the Humpback Whales

Here, in the Atlantic, off the coast
at Provincetown, we've come to see the whales
antic and cavort through the long feast
days of midsummer. Off the boat's prow, schools
of dolphins shimmer and pitch, arched like sails
in the whitecaps, while up on deck, wind-
blown and ruddy, fat as cable spools,
giddy with the songs of humpback whales,

we sight the first spout in the distance
mounting its airy plume toward heaven. Smells
of salt and tuna swim up from the east
as the spokesman for the Cetacean Institute tells
about the invisible drifting nets that spell
trouble for us all, how, entangled, bound
for Mexico to calve, ill-fed, still
giddy with their songs, the humpback whales

will starve. But there, off the bow, our first
humpback is lob-tailing, a gay carousel
of plash and sparkle, while another, flippers poised,
dives deep, and soars up in a breach, the swell
slapping us silly, our large hearts, bell-
like, clanging, our own loud voices finned
with wonder. Our spokesman goes on to tell
us how, giddy with a song, one humpback whale

will teach it to another and another until
the whole great sea is filled with lovely sound.
God give us the good music and the will
to sing along, giddy, with the humpback whales.

5

'O stand, stand at the window
  As the tears scald and start;
You shall love your crooked neighbour
  With your crooked heart.'

Dream Lanes

Not even we four poets could have come up
with a better name for this place—
these brightly lit alleys in which
a fat man in plaid, hipped like a pin,
limping, picks up a seven-ten split;
an old codger, hobbling slow-motion
to the line, knocks off an impossible turkey;
a kid with Down's syndrome, grinning,
his glittery trophies patched to his
jacket, manages, at least once,
to keep the ball in his lane,
as we sing their praises, happy
in our thin Ban-Lon shirts,
each with its singular name.

Would that the world were laid out like this:

where just the right hook or backspin
in the pocket would send problems packing
with that satisfied clack, the music
of marimba and wood block, that sweet percussion;
where, lay it down gently or loft it,
your life would come always back
to pals' catcalls and whistles,
the backslap of spontaneous applause;
where no one would yet have written
the great bowling poem, the poem with
sixteen-pound balls, size nine-and-a-half
shoes, pinsetters dependable as sonnets,
the poem that strikes deep, with no spare words,
the poem with no open frames.

Teachers: A Primer

Mrs. Goldwasser

Shimmered like butterscotch; the sun
had nothing on her. She bangled
when she walked. No one
did not love her. She shone,
she glowed, she lit up any room,
her every gesture jewelry.
And O, when she called us all by name
how we all performed!

Her string of little beads,
her pearls, her rough-cut
gemstones, diamonds, we hung
about her neck. And when
the future pressed her flat,
the world unclasped, and tarnished.

Mrs. Sands

Always dressed in tan. Her voice
abrasive as her name. What choice
did a second grader have? You got
what you got. Her room was hot
but she wore wool and heavy sweat
and worked our childhoods, short and sweet.
You didn't sass her or the school or
she'd rap your knuckles with a ruler.

She had a policy: A tattletale
or liar had to face the wall,
a tail pinned to his sorry ass,

and wear the laughter of the class.
So, to this day, my knuckles bent,
I tell the truth (but tell it slant).

Mrs. Orton

The perennial substitute, like some
obnoxious weed, a European interloper
in our native prairie, her instructions
full of nettles, her gestures parsnip
and burdock. Every day at 3:00 p.m.
we'd dig her out of our small lives,
and every morning she'd pop back.
We prayed she'd get the sack.

And to that end we taunted her—
tacks on her chair, a set-back clock—
as, weeping, she plodded through the week
turning, and turning the other cheek.
And every time we thought that we'd
eradicated her, she'd gone to seed.

Miss Willingham

A Southern Belle, she read *Huck Finn*
aloud to us, dropping her chin
to get the accent right. And me,
for some odd reason, she
singled out to learn the books
of the Bible and recite them back
to her in my high voice
I tried to measure lower. *Nice*

boys go to Sunday School, she said,
and made me promise, when I was grown,
to glorify our heavenly Lord
and take His teaching for my own.
And when she finished that dull story,
she lit out for the territory.

MR. AXT

The basketball coach. Short, tough.
Three days growth on his sharp chin.
Liked to see us all play rough,
and beat up on the stupid, thin,
weak kids who couldn't take it.
He wore white T-shirts, shoes, and slacks,
and taught us all to fake it
if we somehow naturally lacked
the mean competitive spirit.
Once a week he'd have us
bend over and spread our cheeks
for him and old Doc Moffett
who liked to slap us on the butt
and watch as we took leaks.

MRS. REPLOGLE

Her name forbidding, reptilian,
her reputation like a snake
around my expectations.
But then she played *Swan Lake*
and Ferde Grofe's *Grand Canyon Suite,*
a Bach chorale, a Beethoven quartet,

and when we were all back on the street
even the traffic kept a beat.

One day she had us close our eyes
and listen to a symphony
and write whatever image rose
in our small imagination's dark.
And what I saw was poetry,
each note a bird, a flower, a spark.

Mr. Glusenkamp

His gray face was a trapezoid, his voice
droned on like an ellipse.
He hated students and their noise
and loved the full eclipse
of their faces at the end of the day.
No one could have been squarer,
and nothing could have been plainer
than his geometry.

He didn't go for newfangled
stuff—new math, the open classroom.
And yet he taught us angles
and how lines intersect and bloom,
and how infinity was no escape,
and how to give abstractions shape.

Mr. Watts

Sat cross-legged on his desk,
a pretzel of a man, and grinned
as if chemistry were some cosmic joke

and he'd been dealt a hand
of wild cards, all aces.
He drew for us a "ferrous" wheel
and showed when formic acid reverses
HCOOH becomes HOOCH, a peal
of laughter ringing from his nose.
He gave us Avogadro's number
and in his stained lab clothes
formulas for blowing the world asunder
or splitting genes. God knows
why he died shouting "No!" in thunder.

Miss Goff

When Zack Pulanski brought the plastic vomit
and slid it slickly to the vinyl floor
and raised his hand, and her tired eyes fell on it
with horror, the heartless classroom lost in laughter
as the custodian slyly tossed his saw dust on it
and pushed it, grinning, through the door,
she reached into her ancient corner closet
and found some Emily Dickinson mimeos there

which she passed out. And then, herself
passed out on the cold circumference of her desk.
And everybody went their merry ways
but me, who, chancing on one unexpected phrase
after another, sat transfixed until dusk.
Me and Miss Goff, the top of our heads taken off.

In the Cards

Midnight. She complains
in the nursing home they
play too slow, forget what's
led, make up their own rules,
cheat. My grandmother, 89, abloom
in her flower print dress and Ben
Hogan golf cap, her tinted gray
spectacles and cane, her sensible
shoes, reviews the sleepy bidding.
She's waited all year for this:
her children sprawled around her
at the table one last time,
their scores climbing brightly
on the score pad.

Wide awake for once, she exclaims
how she's amazed by each new day,
her one blind eye a pool
of blue glacier water, her other
eye asquint and smiling, her lips
blue in this warm room, taking
tricks for all she's worth.
The evening blurs into beer,
smoke, Velveeta, and sleep.
Oh my, she remarks, *hearts
are trump?* And they are,
and we hold the cards she's dealt us,
and we make our startled bids,
or go over, or go down.

Grandfather, His Book

When my maternal grandfather turned ninety-one,
he took my mother's Underwood and began
to type out the mad story of his life, and,
though he'd never learned to type, roared on
for thirty-some odd days, exhausting one
ream of paper after another, smiling
at the indecipherable gibberish on the page
as if he'd found a reason for his old age.

And if my mother wept, she nevertheless
bound that story together and passed it on
to anyone at the funeral who might one
day make something of it, more or less,
while grandfather lay, smiling at the pews
where all his family sat like good reviews.

Personal Effects

1944. My father, home at last from another war
to end all war, is taking nude photos of my mother.
He does not see us rummaging in the next room,
a half century later, through his personal effects—
law school, multiple sclerosis, son and daughter,
headlines flattened by the press of fifty years—
coming on these negatives that could only be developed
in the heady privacy of his own makeshift darkroom.

My mother gazes out at us, smiling, unembarrassed:
the war is all but over, and everyone survived,
and somewhere in the next room her middle-aged children,
bemused, are gazing back at her immodest love unfurled,
smiling at this side of her they'd never quite imagined,
and God's in His heaven and all's right with the world.

RONALD WALLACE was born in Cedar Rapids, Iowa, in 1945 and grew up in St. Louis, Missouri. The author of nine books of poetry and criticism, he was educated at the College of Wooster and the University of Michigan. His poems have appeared widely in such magazines as *The Atlantic, The Nation, The New Yorker, Poetry,* and *Poetry Northwest.* He directs the creative writing program at the University of Wisconsin, Madison, and serves as editor of the University of Wisconsin Press poetry series. He divides his time between Madison and a forty-acre farm in Bear Valley, Wisconsin.

PITT POETRY SERIES

Ed Ochester, General Editor

Claribel Alegría, *Flowers from the Volcano*
Claribel Alegría, *Woman of the River*
Debra Allbery, *Walking Distance*
Maggie Anderson, *Cold Comfort*
Maggie Anderson, *A Space Filled with Moving*
Robin Becker, *Giacometti's Dog*
Siv Cedering, *Letters from the Floating World*
Lorna Dee Cervantes, *Emplumada*
Robert Coles, *A Festering Sweetness: Poems of American People*
Nancy Vieira Couto, *The Face in the Water*
Jim Daniels, *M-80*
Kate Daniels, *The Niobe Poems*
Kate Daniels, *The White Wave*
Toi Derricotte, *Captivity*
Sharon Doubiago, *South America Mi Hija*
Stuart Dybek, *Brass Knuckles*
Odysseus Elytis, *The Axion Esti*
Jane Flanders, *Timepiece*
Forrest Gander, *Lynchburg*
Richard Garcia, *The Flying Garcias*
Suzanne Gardinier, *The New World*
Gary Gildner, *Blue Like the Heavens: New & Selected Poems*
Elton Glaser, *Color Photographs of the Ruins*
Hunt Hawkins, *The Domestic Life*
Lawrence Joseph, *Curriculum Vitae*
Lawrence Joseph, *Shouting at No One*
Julia Kasdorf, *Sleeping Preacher*
Etheridge Knight, *The Essential Etheridge Knight*
Bill Knott, *Poems, 1963–1988*
Ted Kooser, *One World at a Time*
Ted Kooser, *Sure Signs: New and Selected Poems*
Ted Kooser, *Weather Central*
Larry Levis, *The Widening Spell of the Leaves*
Larry Levis, *Winter Stars*
Larry Levis, *Wrecking Crew*
Irene McKinney, *Six O'Clock Mine Report*
Archibald MacLeish, *The Great American Fourth of July Parade*

Peter Meinke, *Liquid Paper: New and Selected Poems*
Peter Meinke, *Night Watch on the Chesapeake*
Carol Muske, *Applause*
Carol Muske, *Wyndmere*
Leonard Nathan, *Carrying On: New & Selected Poems*
Ed Ochester and Peter Oresick, *The Pittsburgh Book of
    Contemporary American Poetry*
Sharon Olds, *Satan Says*
Alicia Suskin Ostriker, *Green Age*
Alicia Suskin Ostriker, *The Imaginary Lover*
Greg Pape, *Black Branches*
Greg Pape, *Storm Pattern*
Kathleen Peirce, *Mercy*
David Rivard, *Torque*
Liz Rosenberg, *Children of Paradise*
Liz Rosenberg, *The Fire Music*
Natasha Sajé, *Red Under the Skin*
Maxine Scates, *Toluca Street*
Richard Shelton, *Selected Poems, 1969–1981*
Reginald Shepherd, *Some Are Drowning*
Betsy Sholl, *The Red Line*
Peggy Shumaker, *The Circle of Totems*
Peggy Shumaker, *Wings Moist from the Other World*
Jeffrey Skinner, *The Company of Heaven*
Cathy Song, *School Figures*
Leslie Ullman, *Dreams by No One's Daughter*
Constance Urdang, *Alternative Lives*
Constance Urdang, *Only the World*
Michael Van Walleghen, *Tall Birds Stalking*
Ronald Wallace, *People and Dog in the Sun*
Ronald Wallace, *Time's Fancy*
Belle Waring, *Refuge*
Michael S. Weaver, *My Father's Geography*
Robley Wilson, *Kingdoms of the Ordinary*
Robley Wilson, *A Pleasure Tree*
David Wojahn, *Glassworks*
David Wojahn, *Late Empire*
David Wojahn, *Mystery Train*
Paul Zimmer, *Family Reunion: Selected and New Poems*